First Questions and Answers about **Water**

Do Fish Drink?

TIME
LIFE *for*
Children®

ALEXANDRIA, VIRGINIA

Contents

Why do I have to take a bath?

How many things can you find in this picture that have to do with water?

You take baths to wash off dirt so you'll look and smell clean. You also take baths to scrub off germs. Germs are too tiny to see, but they are on everything you touch, and they stay on your skin. Some germs can make you sick. So you need to wash even if you don't feel dirty.

R-r-ribbit!

How does soap make bubbles?

You can't see it, but water has a kind of thin covering on its top like the outside of a balloon. Soap makes the covering stretchy. When air gets underneath the water, the covering stretches and holds the air inside. That makes bubbles. It's like blowing up tiny balloons.

Where does the dirty water go?

Can you follow the pipes from the bathtub and toilet and washing machine with your finger?
They all go to the same place!

Away to get clean again! All the water from bathtubs, dishwashers, sinks, and toilets goes down drains and into thin pipes in the floors and walls. A bigger pipe carries this wastewater away from the house. In most towns, it goes to an even bigger pipe under the street, called a sewer. The sewer carries wastewater from other houses to a place where it all gets cleaned.

How does the dirty water get cleaned?

Dirty water is cleaned at a group of buildings called a wastewater treatment plant. Most of the time the plant is near a river, and it's a very busy place.

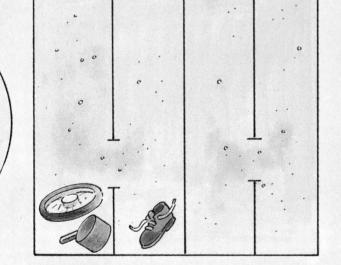

First, the dirty water runs through bars that trap big pieces of garbage.

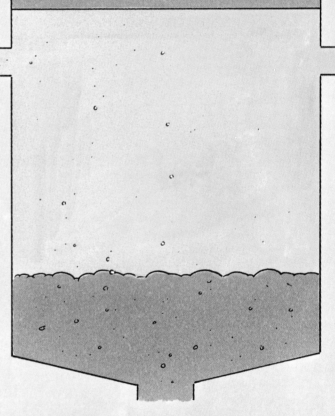

Next the water is left in a pool, where some of the dirt sinks to the bottom.

The water from the top of the pool then flows into a large pond with tiny, tiny bugs that eat the rest of the dirt.

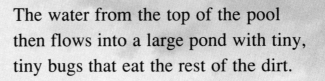

Finally, the water is sent into the river. The water isn't clean enough for people to drink, but it is clean enough for fish and other animals.

Who lives in the river?

All kinds of animals live in or near rivers.
Each one uses the water in its own
special way, day and night.

At the end
of the day,
deer come
to drink.

Water striders' feet
spread out so they can
walk right on top
of the water.

Dragonflies lay their eggs
in the water.

Raccoons come at night
to hunt insects and fish.

Father **sunfish** watch over
their nests until the eggs hatch.

Catfish have whiskers
that help them find food.

Herons use their long beaks to fish near the shore.

Beavers build their houses on the edge of the river.

*Guess what we **tadpoles** will be when we grow up!*

Crayfish hide under stones so they won't get eaten or swept away by the river's flow.

Turtles lie in the sun and slide into the water to find food.

How does a tadpole turn into a frog?

Tadpoles hatch from eggs that mother frogs lay in the water. They look like tiny fish, wiggling their tails to swim. As they get older, their tails get smaller, and front and back legs begin to grow. Finally, the tails disappear. Then the animals leap out of the water as grown-up frogs, ready to catch bugs with their long tongues!

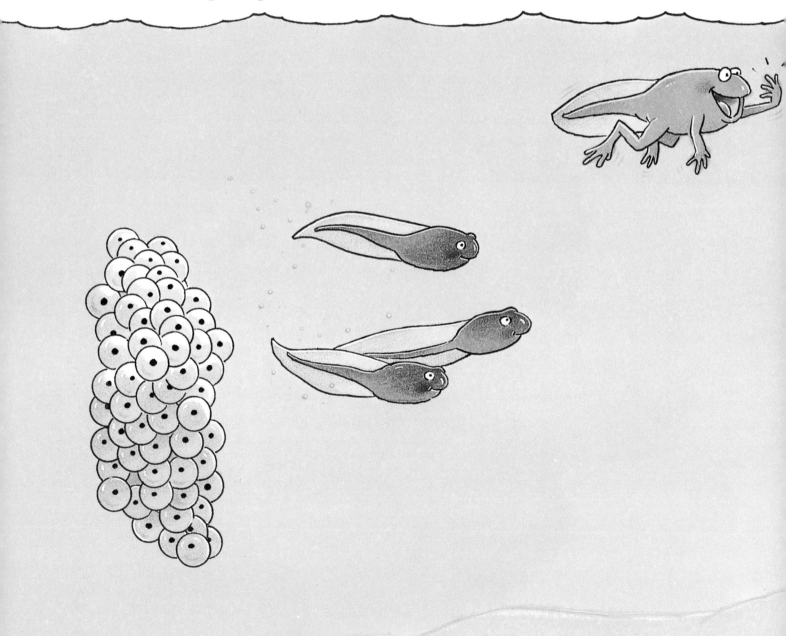

Did you know?

On warm nights, male frogs sing to female frogs. They puff out their throats and

CROAK!

Different frogs make different sounds. Spring peepers sound like jingling bells. A green frog makes a deep R-r-ribbit!

Do fish drink?

Fish in rivers, ponds, and streams drink just a little water. They swallow some when they open their mouths to eat. So they drink and eat at the same time! Water also oozes into their bodies through tiny holes in their skin.

How do fish stay underwater?

When you take a breath, the air goes into your chest to your lungs. Your lungs use something called oxygen that is in the air. Fish use oxygen, too. But they don't have to come up to breathe! Instead of lungs, they have gills, which are slits behind their eyes. Gills take oxygen right out of the water. Gills work only in the water, though: A fish would die if it stayed out in the air too long.

Did you know?

A diving suit lets you breathe underwater. It has tanks of air that you wear on your back. A hose carries the air from the tanks to your mouth.

I don't have gills. I stay underwater a long time by holding my breath.

Can you find the gills on the catfish?

19

Why do ducks have webbed feet?

Ducks have thick, tough skin, called webbing, that stretches between their toes. They use their webbed feet like paddles to push them through the water, just as people use flippers to help them swim. A webbed foot can push a lot more water than a bird's foot without webbing.

I have webbed feet, too, which make me a great swimmer.

Did you know?

A duck's feathers are covered with a special oil that keeps the duck dry. Water rolls right off the duck's back, so it doesn't get wet.

Why do boats float?

When a boat is put into a river or lake, it pushes water down and to the side to make room for itself. Boats are built to be lighter than the water they push aside. But if too many people or things are put on a boat, it becomes heavier than the water it has pushed out of its way. Then watch out—the boat will sink!

Try it!

Put some water in a bowl and see which floats best: a crayon, a penny, or a leaf. Try other things. Guess why some objects float better than others. **Adults always should supervise children with small objects.**

Where do rivers go?

Little streams on hills or mountains join together
to make big rivers. Rivers flow downhill, joining other
streams along the way and growing wider. Most rivers
flow all the way to the ocean. But some rivers go to
big lakes, which in turn empty into rivers to the ocean.

Did you know?

Water *always* flows downhill!
Next time it rains, watch
the water as it streams along
the sidewalk. Does it run
from the top to the bottom?

Why does the ocean taste salty, but rivers don't?

On their way to the ocean, rivers pick up salt from rocks and soil that have salt in them. River water empties the salt into the ocean, which stays salty because the ocean doesn't flow anywhere. But rivers stay fresh because they keep getting new water from rain and streams to wash the salt to the ocean.

I'm going to find fresh water. See you later.

Did you know?

Creatures that live in and near the ocean can drink salt water because they're used to it. But if you tried that, you'd get sick. It's too salty for people to drink.

Who lives in the ocean?

Crabs keep safe from enemies inside a hard shell. When they get too big for their shells, they climb out and grow new ones.

Pelicans have wide, deep beaks like soup ladles to scoop up fish in the water.

Flounders live in shallow water near the sandy shore. Their light color mixes in with sand and stones so enemies can't see them.

Sea horses curl their tails around seaweed like monkeys hanging on to tree branches.

Most of the world is covered by ocean, so there's plenty of room for all kinds of wonderful creatures to live together.

Flying fish jump out of the ocean and keep right on going! Their fins spread out like wings so they can soar away from danger.

Whales are the largest creatures in the world. They look like fish, but they're not. They come to the surface to breathe air.

Herrings swim in groups called schools.

Octopuses squirt black ink and disappear in a dark cloud to get away from danger.

29

How deep is the ocean?

It's so deep that whole mountains can fit underwater without sticking out! The deepest part of the ocean is far, far away from the beach. At the very bottom, it's dark and cold, because sunlight can't shine all the way down through so much water.

Did you know?

There are sea creatures that live only in the deepest, darkest part of the ocean. Some of them are like underwater fireflies. They have rows of lights that flash in the dark.

Why doesn't the ocean overflow?

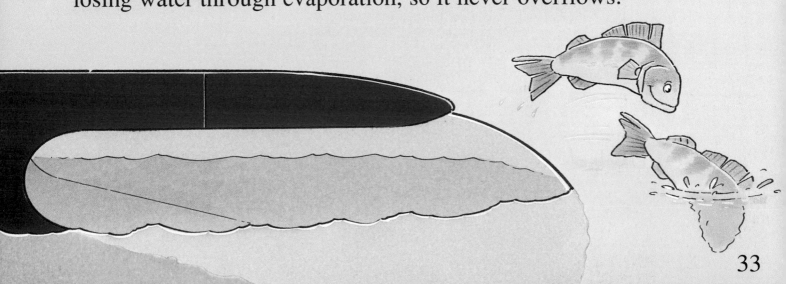

River water flows into oceans all the time. But the sun's heat turns ocean water into millions of invisible little drops, called water vapor, that rise into the air. When water changes into water vapor, we call this evaporation. The ocean is always losing water through evaporation, so it never overflows.

Where does rain come from?

Water vapor rises into the sky, where the air is colder than below. The cold makes the tiny water drops join together into bigger, heavier drops. The drops aren't invisible now—they've become clouds. When clouds get too full of these big heavy drops, they break apart and fall to the ground as raindrops.

How do my clothes dry?

Anything that's wet loses water through evaporation—evaporation is just a big word for drying. Water evaporates from oceans, pitchers of lemonade, and your wet clothes. Drying can take a long time, but heat and moving air speed it up. That's why clothes dry faster in a clothes dryer or outside on a sunny, breezy day.

Why do I get thirsty?

Your body needs water to keep healthy and help change food into energy. In fact, you need about four glasses of water every day, and even more when it's hot outside. So feeling thirsty is your body's way of sending you a message: More water, please!

How does water turn into ice?

Water changes shape like magic, depending on how hot or cold it is. When it's not too hot and not too cold, it's a liquid that we can pour and drink or wash with. When it's heated, it becomes steam, or water vapor. And when water becomes very cold, it turns into ice. When ice gets warm, it melts again!

Try it!

Ice melts faster in a warm place than in a cold place. With an adult's help, place an ice cube in a bowl in the refrigerator. Put another one in a bowl on the counter. Which one melts faster?

Does everything need to drink water?

Every living thing needs water, but some plants and animals don't need as much as others. It almost never rains in the desert, so plants and animals there have learned to live with very little water. They save every drop they can.

A **cactus** saves water inside its thick skin. Sharp needles keep thirsty animals from sucking it out.

Desert **lizards** never drink water. They get all the water they need from the insects and plants that they eat.

Camels can drink up to 30 gallons of water all at once. That's enough for 480 glasses. Then they go for a week without a drop.

43

How does the water get hot?

Clean, cold water comes into the house through pipes. Some goes straight to the cold-water faucets. The rest goes to a water heater. This is like a big pot that cooks the water until it's hot. Pipes carry the heated water to the hot-water faucet in your sink or tub.

The water can get really hot, so don't ever turn it on yourself.

Is there enough water for everyone?

There's the same amount of water in the world now as always, but there are many more people now than there used to be. And people today use much more water than people did long ago. We must use water carefully so everyone gets as much as he or she needs.

Did you know?

There are lots of ways you and your family can save water. Here are three of them:

1. Turn off the faucet while you brush your teeth. You'll save enough water each time to fill 80 glasses!

2. Don't fill your tub to the top. If you shower, make it a short one.

3. Always turn off the water all the way when you finish using it.

TIME-LIFE for CHILDREN ®

President: Robert H. Smith
Associate Publisher/Managing Editor: Neil Kagan
Assistant Managing Editor: Patricia Daniels
Editorial Directors: Jean Burke Crawford, Allan Fallow,
        Karin Kinney, Sara Mark, Elizabeth Ward
Director of Marketing: Margaret Mooney
Product Managers: Cassandra Ford, Amy Haworth,
        Shelley L. Schimkus
Director of Finance: Lisa Peterson
Publishing Assistant: Marike van der Veen
Administrative Assistant: Barbara A. Jones
Production Manager: Marlene Zack
Senior Copy Coordinator: Colette Stockum
Production: Celia Beattie
Supervisor of Quality Control: James King
Assistant Supervisor of
 Quality Control: Miriam P. Newton
Library: Louise D. Forstall

Special Contributor: Barbara Klein
Researcher: Jocelyn Lindsay
Writer: Jacqueline A. Ball

Designed by	David Bennett Books
Series design	David Bennett
Book design	Andrew Crowson
Art direction	David Bennett & Andrew Crowson
Illustrated by	Stuart Trotter
Additional cover illustrations by	Malcolm Livingstone

First printing. Printed in U.S.A.
Published simultaneously in Canada.

Time Life Inc. is a wholly owned subsidiary of THE TIME INC. BOOK COMPANY.

TIME-LIFE is a trademark of Time Warner Inc. U.S.A.

For subscription information, call 1-800-621-7026.

Library of congress Cataloging-in-Publication Data
Do fish Drink? : first questions and answers about water.
p. cm. — (Library of first questions and answers)
Summary : Discusses, in question-and-answer format, the sources,
cycle, and uses of water, why oceans are salty, and other related topics.
ISBN O— 7835 —0850—6
1. Water—Juvenile literature. (1. Water— Miscellaneous.
2. Questions and answers.) I. Time— Life for Children (Firm) II. Series.
GB662. 3. D6 1993
553. 7— dc20
92— 40301
CIP
AC

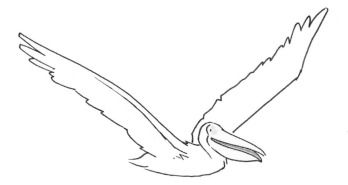

Consultants

Dr. Lewis P. Lipsitt, an internationally recognized specialist on childhood development, was the 1990 recipient of the Nicholas Hobbs Award for science in the service of children. He has served as the science director for the American Psychological Association and is a professor of psychology and medical science at Brown University, where he is director of the Child Study Center.

Thomas D. Mullin directs the Hidden Oaks Nature Center in Fairfax County, Virginia, where he coordinates workshops and seminars designed to promote appreciation for wildlife and the environment. He is also the Washington representative for the National Association for Interpretation, a professional organization for naturalists involved in public education.

Dr. Judith A. Schickedanz, an authority on the education of preschool children, is an associate professor of early childhood education at the Boston University School of Education, where she also directs the Early Childhood Learning Laboratory. Her published work includes *More Than the ABC's: Early Stages of Reading and Writing Development* as well as several textbooks and many scholarly papers.